Contents

CW00350363

DO NOT PHOTOCOPY © MUSIC

Introduction

Welcome to *Music Theory in Practice Model Answers*, Grade 5. These answers are a useful resource to help you prepare for ABRSM Theory of Music exams. This book is designed to be used alongside the revised *Music Theory in Practice* workbook (published 2008).

All the answers in this book would receive full marks in an exam. Accepted options are included for cases where an answer may be expressed in more than one way. For composition-style questions, a model answer is provided as an example of good practice.

Using these answers

- Answers are given in the same order and, where possible, in the same layout as in the corresponding *Music Theory in Practice* workbook. This makes it easy to match the answers to the questions.
- Where it is necessary to show the answer on a stave, the original stave is printed in grey with the answer shown in black, for example:

- Alternative answers are separated by an oblique stroke (/) or by *or*, for example:

B / B♮ / B natural

- Answers that require the candidate to write out a scale or chord have been shown at one octave only. Reasonable alternatives at different octaves can also receive full marks.

First published in 2009 by ABRSM (Publishing) Ltd, a wholly owned subsidiary of ABRSM
Reprinted in 2010, 2012, 2013, 2015, 2016, 2018

© 2009 by The Associated Board of the Royal Schools of Music

Typeset by Barnes Music Engraving Ltd
Cover by Økvik Design
Inside design by Vermillion
Printed in England by Caligraving Ltd, Thetford, Norfolk,
on materials from sustainable sources

Irregular time signatures

Tenor clef

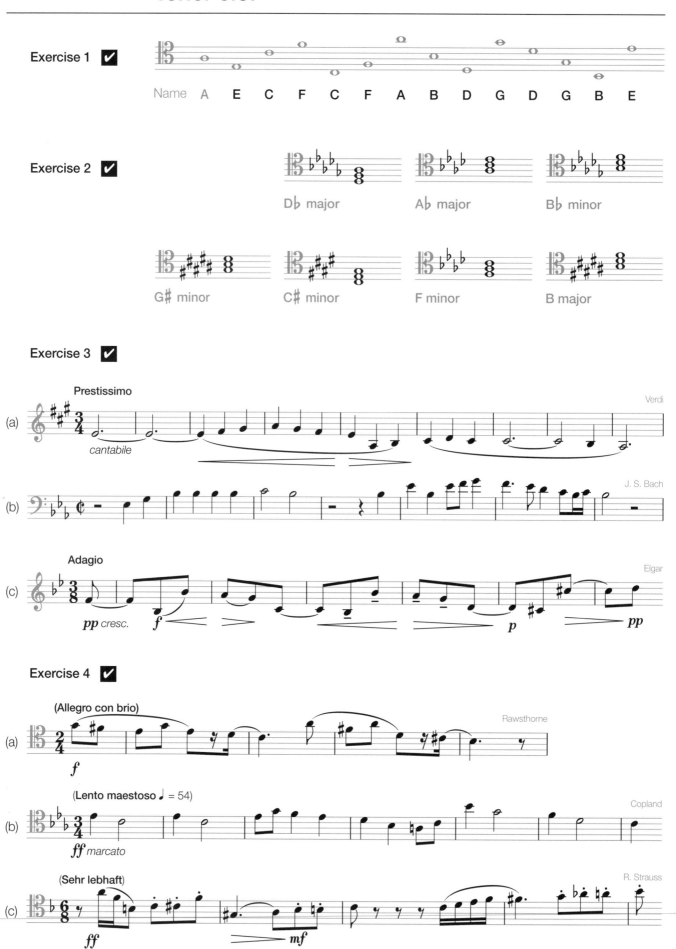

Exercise 1 ✔

Name A E C F C F A B D G D G B E

Exercise 2 ✔

Db major   Ab major   Bb minor

G# minor   C# minor   F minor   B major

Exercise 3 ✔

(a) Prestissimo — Verdi
cantabile

(b) — J. S. Bach

(c) Adagio — Elgar
pp cresc.   f   p   pp

Exercise 4 ✔

(a) (Allegro con brio) — Rawsthorne
f

(b) (Lento maestoso ♩ = 54) — Copland
ff marcato

(c) (Sehr lebhaft) — R. Strauss
ff   mf

Major and minor keys up to six sharps and flats

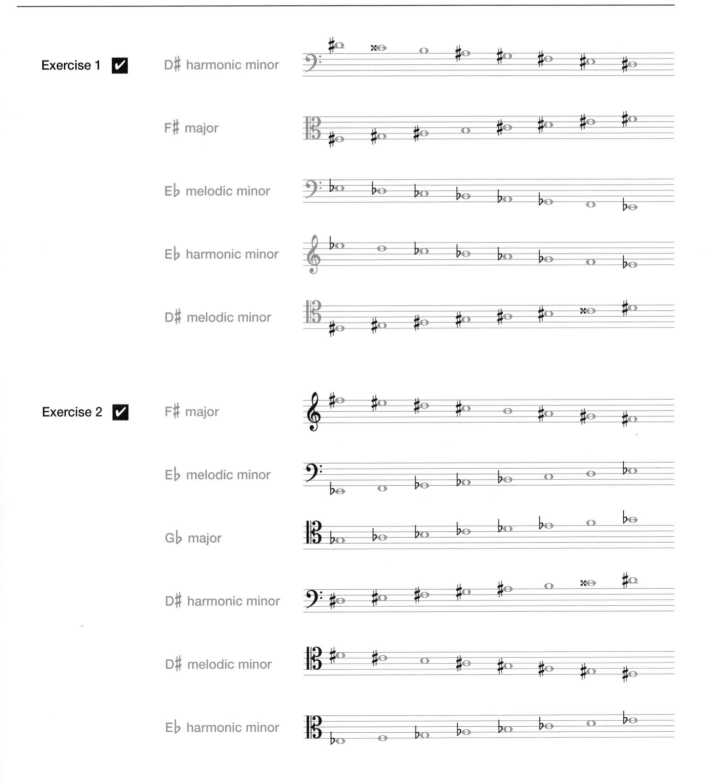

Exercise 1 ✔

D♯ harmonic minor

F♯ major

E♭ melodic minor

E♭ harmonic minor

D♯ melodic minor

Exercise 2 ✔

F♯ major

E♭ melodic minor

G♭ major

D♯ harmonic minor

D♯ melodic minor

E♭ harmonic minor

Exercise 3 ☑

F♯ major

D♯ minor

G♭ major

E♭ minor

Key **D♯ minor**

Exercise 4 ☑ (a)

J. S. Bach

Key **F♯ major**

Allegro giusto

(b)

Tchaikovsky

Key **E♭ minor**

Moderato

(c)

Rachmaninoff

Key **G♭ major**

Andante molto calmo

(d)

Puccini

Exercise 5 ✔

(i)

(ii)

Transposition

Exercise 1 ✔

Exercise 2 ✔

8

Voices in score

Exercise 1 ✔

J. S. Bach

Exercise 2 ✔

More irregular time divisions

Exercise 1 ✔

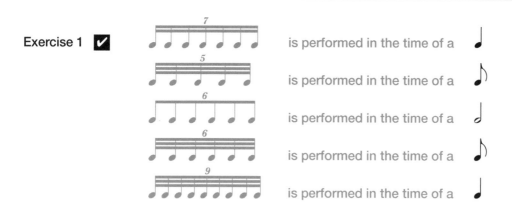

is performed in the time of a ♩

is performed in the time of a ♪

is performed in the time of a 𝅗𝅥

is performed in the time of a ♪

is performed in the time of a ♩

Exercise 2 ✔

Intervals

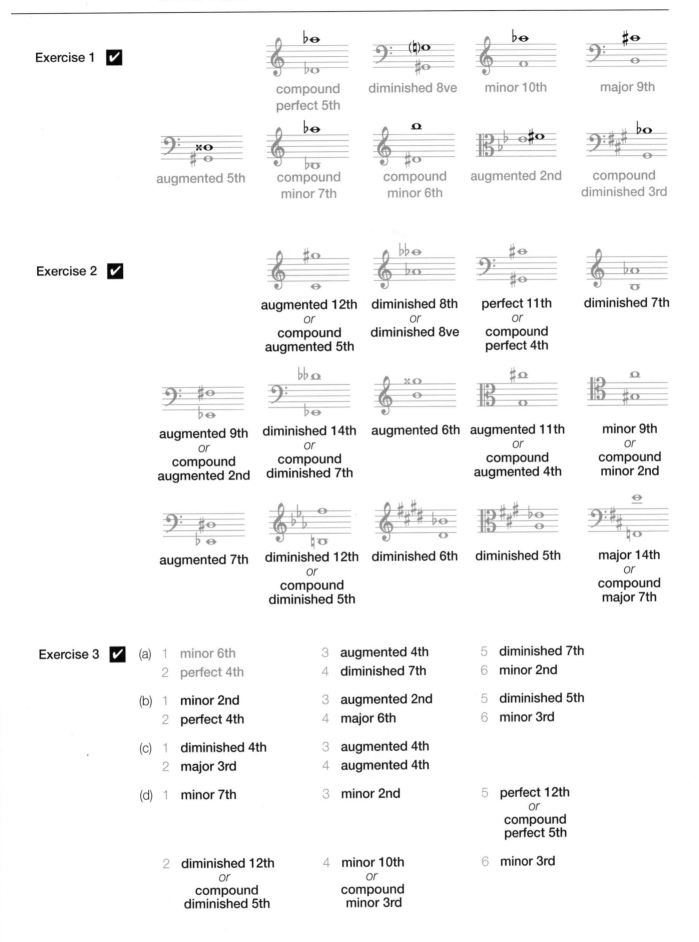

Exercise 3 (a)   1   minor 6th   3   augmented 4th   5   diminished 7th

                2   perfect 4th   4   diminished 7th   6   minor 2nd

        (b)   1   minor 2nd   3   augmented 2nd   5   diminished 5th

                2   perfect 4th   4   major 6th   6   minor 3rd

        (c)   1   diminished 4th   3   augmented 4th

                2   major 3rd   4   augmented 4th

        (d)   1   minor 7th   3   minor 2nd   5   perfect 12th
                                                                          or
                                                               compound
                                                               perfect 5th

                2   diminished 12th   4   minor 10th   6   minor 3rd
                       or   *or*
                   compound   compound
                  diminished 5th   minor 3rd

Exercise 4 ✔   1 perfect 5th   3 minor 7th   5 major 9th
                                                                  or
                                                                  compound
                                                                  major 2nd

                2 major 6th   4 diminished 5th   6 perfect 11th
                                                                  or
                                                                  compound
                                                                  perfect 4th

Naming chords

Exercise 1 ✔ (a) C major   Vb   Ib   II   Ic

            (b) F major   I   IIb   IVb   Vb

            (c) B minor   I   Vb   IVb   IIb   V

            (d) D major   I   Ib   Vb   IIb   Ic   V

            (e) B♭ major   Vb   IVb   Ic   V

            (f) C minor   V   IV   II   I

            (g) E♭ major   Ib   Vb   II   IVb

Composing a melody

Exercise 1 ✔   There are many ways of completing this exercise. The specimen answers that follow provide
                     examples of good practice.

(a) Oboe — Moderato espressivo — *mp*

(b) Oboe — Allegretto con moto — *mp* — *mf* — *f*

(j) Trombone — Allegro ma non troppo

(k) Violin — Andantino

(l) Trumpet — Calypso feel

(m) Bassoon — Moderato con anima

Exercise 2 ✔ There are many ways of completing this exercise. The specimen answers that follow provide examples of good practice.

Words by Robert Louis Stevenson

(a) Andante

But slum - ber hold me tight - ly till I wak - en in the dawn, ___ And hear the thrush - es sing - ing, thrush - es sing - ing in the li - lacs round the lawn.

18 |

Allegretto

Words by Sacheverell Sitwell

(l)

This is Where the ri - ver Runs down to the sea,___ Lis - ten to its mu - sic,

hear this mys-te - ry! Lis-ten to its mu - sic,___ hear this_ mys - te - ry!

Ornaments

Exercise 1 ✔

(a) *(Presto)* — Haydn

(b) *(Allegretto)* — Schubert

(c) *(Allegretto)* — Mozart

(d) **Allegro cantabile** — Widor

Chords at cadential points

Exercise 1 ✔ For the Grade 5 Theory Exam, candidates do not have to indicate the position of chords or state which note is in the bass.

(a) 1 Chord: ____ / IV / C major   2 Chord: ____ / I / G major

3 Chord: ____ / I / G major   4 Chord: ____ / V / D major

(b) 1 Chord: ____ / II / E minor   2 Chord: ____ / V / A major

3 Chord: ____ / V / A major   4 Chord: ____ / I / D major

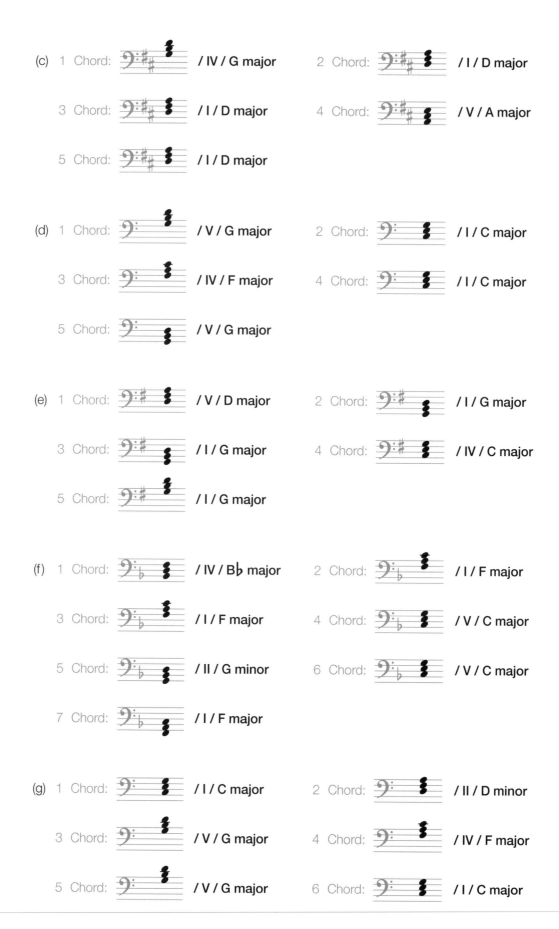

(c) 1 Chord: / IV / G major   2 Chord: / I / D major

3 Chord: / I / D major   4 Chord: / V / A major

5 Chord: / I / D major

(d) 1 Chord: / V / G major   2 Chord: / I / C major

3 Chord: / IV / F major   4 Chord: / I / C major

5 Chord: / V / G major

(e) 1 Chord: / V / D major   2 Chord: / I / G major

3 Chord: / I / G major   4 Chord: / IV / C major

5 Chord: / I / G major

(f) 1 Chord: / IV / B♭ major   2 Chord: / I / F major

3 Chord: / I / F major   4 Chord: / V / C major

5 Chord: / II / G minor   6 Chord: / V / C major

7 Chord: / I / F major

(g) 1 Chord: / I / C major   2 Chord: / II / D minor

3 Chord: / V / G major   4 Chord: / IV / F major

5 Chord: / V / G major   6 Chord: / I / C major

Exercise 1 ✔ (a) piano

use of sustaining pedal / usual piano layout of two staves

(b) G♭ major

(c) **4th** and **7th**

(d) minor 2nd   major 2nd   minor 3rd   major 3rd   perfect 4th   perfect 5th

| | ✔ | ✔ | | ✔ | |

(e) I / tonic chord

(f) pedal like this all the way through / go on pedalling in the same way / the pedalling in bar 1 should continue in a similar manner throughout

(g) ♩ = 72–92

(h)

Exercise 2 ✔ (a) Ic / tonic chord in second inversion

(b) Bar 2 **major 2nd**   Bar 3 **perfect 5th**   Bar 4 **major 3rd**
Bar 5 **minor 3rd**   Bar 6 **augmented 2nd**

(c) **forced / accented**

(d) **turn**

(e)

(f) **bassoon / double bassoon**

(g) **double reed**

(h)

Exercise 3 ✔ (a) Soprano, Alto, Tenor, Bass

(b)

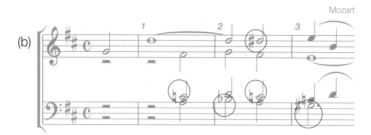

Mozart

(c) **major 9th / compound major 2nd**

(d) **octave / perfect ovtave**

(e) **major 2nd**

(f) (i) **Ib**
   (ii) **IVb**
   (iii) **Ic**

(g) **D**

(h) any two of the following instruments could play the melody at sounding pitch:
   cello / double bass / French horn / bassoon / trombone / bass trombone

(i)

Exercise 4 ☑   (a) quintuple

(b) 1st violin / first violin / violin I
2nd violin / second violin / violin II
viola
violoncello / cello

(c) (i)   lively
(ii)   forced / accented
(iii) pluck the strings

(d) play as semiquavers

(e) (i)   perfect 5th
(ii)   major 6th
(iii) augmented 4th

(f) to remind players that accidentals only refer to a particular octave / to assure the 1st
violin player of the intentional clash (of a diminished octave) with another part

(g)

Acknowledgements

Page 3: d'Indy, *Du Rythme*, Op. 68 No. 10
Reproduced by permission of Editions Henn, Switzerland / United Music Publishers Ltd.

Page 3: Prokofiev, Piano Sonata No. 7 (3rd mvt)
© Copyright 1943 Boosey & Hawkes Music Publishers Ltd for the UK, British
Commonwealth (Ex Canada), Eire & South Africa
Reproduced by permission of Boosey & Hawkes Music Publishers Ltd.

Page 3: Stravinsky, *Petrouchka* ('Masqueraders')
© Copyright 1912 by Hawkes & Son (London) Ltd
Reproduced by permission of Boosey & Hawkes Music Publishers Ltd

Page 3: Holst, *The Planets* ('Mars')
© Copyright 1921 F&B Goodwin Ltd. Transferred to J. Curwen & Sons Ltd
All rights reserved. Reproduced for sale in France, Spain, Italy & Mexico by permission
of Music Sales Ltd.

Page 3: Shostakovich, String Quartet No. 2 (2nd mvt)
© Copyright 1944 Boosey & Hawkes Music Publishers Ltd for the UK, British
Commonwealth (Ex Canada), Eire & South Africa
Reproduced by permission of Boosey & Hawkes Music Publishers Ltd.

Page 3: Stravinsky, Octet for Wind Instruments (2nd mvt)
© Copyright 1927 Hawkes & Son (London) Ltd.
Revised version © 1952 Hawkes & Son (London) Ltd
Reproduced by permission of Boosey & Hawkes Music Publishers Ltd.

Page 3: Copland, Duo for Flute and Piano (2nd mvt)
© Copyright 1971 The Aaron Copland Fund for Music, Inc.
Boosey & Hawkes, Inc. sole licensee
Reproduced by permission of Boosey & Hawkes Music Publishers Ltd.

Page 4: Elgar, Cello Concerto (3rd mvt)
© Copyright 1919 Novello & Co. Ltd
All rights reserved. Reproduced for sale in France, Spain, Italy & Mexico
by permission of Novello & Co. Ltd.

Page 4: Rawsthorne, *Street Corner* (Overture)
© Oxford University Press 1949. Extract reproduced by permission. All rights reserved.

Page 4: Copland, *Billy the Kid* (Intro: 'The open prairie')
© Copyright 1978 The Aaron Copland Fund for Music, Inc.
Boosey & Hawkes, Inc. sole licensee
Reproduced by permission of Boosey & Hawkes Music Publishers Ltd.

Page 4: R. Strauss, *Till Eulenspiegel*
© 1895 Josef Aibl Musikverlag. Copyright assigned 1932 to C. F. Peters
Reproduced by permission.

Page 6: Rachmaninoff, *Élégie*, Op. 3 No.1
© Copyright 1893 Hawkes & Son (London) Ltd
Reproduced by permission of Boosey & Hawkes Music Publishers Ltd.

Page 8: Dukas, *The Sorcerer's Apprentice*
Reproduced by permission of Editions Durand S. A., Paris.

Page 8: Gershwin, *An American in Paris*
© 1929 WB MUSIC CORP.
All rights reserved.
An AMERICAN IN PARIS™ is a trademark of the George Gershwin Family Trust.
GERSHWIN® and GEORGE GERSHWIN® are registered trademarks of Gershwin Enterprises.
Used by permission.

Page 8: Elgar, *2nd Wand of Youth Suite* ('The Wild Bears')
© Copyright 1907 Novello & Co. Ltd
All rights reserved. Reproduced for sale in France, Spain, Italy & Mexico
by permission of Novello & Co. Ltd.

Page 9: Elgar, *Pomp and Circumstance* March No. 1
Reproduced for sale in France, Spain & Mexico by permission of
Boosey & Hawkes Music Publishers Ltd.

Page 9: Bliss, Clarinet Quintet (1st mvt)
© Copyright 1933 Novello & Co. Ltd
All rights reserved. International copyright secured. Reproduced by permission.

Page 9: Ravel, *Le Tombeau de Couperin* (Forlane)
Reproduced for sale in France, Belgium, Italy & Spain by permission of Editions
Durand S. A., Paris / Universal Music Publishing MGB Ltd.

Page 9: Britten, *War Requiem* (Offertorium)
© Copyright 1961 Boosey & Hawkes Music Publishers Ltd
Reproduced by permission of Boosey & Hawkes Music Publishers Ltd.

Page 10: Elgar, *Falstaff*
© Copyright 1913 Novello & Co. Ltd
All rights reserved. Reproduced for sale in France, Spain, Italy & Mexico
by permission of Novello & Co. Ltd.

Page 10: Rachmaninoff, Piano Concerto No. 1 (3rd mvt)
© 1921 Boosey & Hawkes Music Publishers Ltd
Reproduced by permission of Boosey & Hawkes Music Publishers Ltd.

Page 10: Sibelius, Symphony No. 2 (2nd mvt)
© Breitkopf & Härtel, Wiesbaden

Page 10: Delius, *Walk to the Paradise Garden*
Reproduced for sale in France, Spain & Mexico by permission of
Boosey & Hawkes Music Publishers Ltd.

Page 12: Vaughan Williams, Symphony No. 4 (1st mvt)
© Oxford University Press 1935. Extract reproduced by permission. All rights reserved.

Page 12: Britten, *Serenade for tenor, horn & strings* ('Dirge')
© Copyright 1944 Hawkes & Son (London) Ltd
Reproduced by permission of Boosey & Hawkes Music Publishers Ltd.

Page 12: Walton, Symphony No. 1 (1st mvt)
© Oxford University Press 1936. Extract reproduced by permission. All rights reserved.

Page 19: Sacheverell Sitwell Poem
Extract from Grande Sicilienne from The Collected Poems by Sacheverell Sitwell
© Sacheverell Sitwell reprinted by permission of Peters Fraser & Dunlop
(www.petersfraserdunlop.com) on behalf of the Estate of Sacheverell Sitwell.

Page 19: Widor, Organ Symphony No. 5
Reproduced by permission of Editions Hamelle, Paris / United Music
Publishers Ltd.

Page 23: Ravel, String Quartet
Reproduced for sale in France, Belgium, Italy & Spain by permission of Editions
Durand S. A., Paris / Universal Music Publishers MGB Ltd.